JAMES

MORE GRACE

10 Publishing
a division of **10** of those.com

Copyright © 2018 by Julia Marsden

First published in Great Britain in 2018

British Library Cataloguing in Publication Data
A record for this book is available from the British Library

ISBN: 978-1-912373-15-4
Designed by Diane Warnes
Printed in the UK

10Publishing, a division of 10ofthose.com
Unit C, Tomlinson Road, Leyland, PR25 2DY, England
Email: info@10ofthose.com
Website: www.10ofthose.com

J. Marsden

40 UNDATED DEVOTIONS THROUGH THE BOOK OF JAMES

Some letters are hard to write. Writing hard truths to loved ones can be especially difficult.

The letter we are going to read might well have been a hard letter to write and perhaps an even harder one to receive. It is full of searching challenges and, at times, painful rebukes. Yet, it is also full of love and concern. As we read it, we will need to listen out for the challenges but also for the loving care. Sometimes love has to be tough. We need tough love at times to call us back from danger and to keep us on the right track. This part of God's word is powerful to do both. James wanted those things for his first readers. Let's pray that this letter does those things for us too.

- **How does James choose to introduce himself (1:1)?**

Early church tradition suggests that the James who wrote this letter was the half-brother of the Lord Jesus himself. This James became the first leader of the church in Jerusalem. It was a senior and influential position.

But James himself doesn't mention any of this. He doesn't mention anything that would make him seem important and special, although he probably could have. James introduces himself as a servant. He is 'a servant of God and of the Lord Jesus Christ'. That could be a description of any Christian.

James will have a lot to say in his letter about being humble. He will call his readers to humble themselves again before their Lord. Here in 1:1 we learn that when James later says, 'Humble yourselves' (4:10), he is asking his readers to do what he himself has already done. He has humbled himself before God and before the Lord Jesus, and become their servant.

James is a servant on his masters' business. His words, painful as they may be to hear at times, are written at his Lord's bidding. He is bringing his readers what God and the Lord Jesus Christ want to say to them, and it is important that his readers and we know that.

PRAY

Ask God to help you respond humbly and obediently to the challenges of James' letter.

James writes as a humble servant of his Lord. But who is he addressing?

As we read on, it seems that James is writing to one particular congregation that he knows well. It is true that James tends to speak truths in pithy general terms – that is his style. But every so often it becomes obvious that James is writing to one specific church family, for he clearly knows all about their particular issues and problems.

For example, '... you have dishonoured the poor' (2:6), James writes. James also knows the details of how rich people are currently oppressing these believers by exploiting them, dragging them into court and blaspheming the name of Christ (2:6–7). James knows too about certain wealthy landowners who are failing to pay the wages of the workers who have mowed their fields (5:4).

Perhaps most revealing of all, James tells this congregation, 'Not many of you should become teachers' (3:1). This is not standard New Testament advice to believers. There is something clearly very wrong with this church and James knows about it.

• *Interestingly, what are the first two things James says about these believers (1:1)?*

In Old Testament times, God chose a nation made up of twelve tribes to be his own people. Now God's people are made up of all those who believe in Jesus; every Christian is a member of the 'twelve tribes' now. And we are certainly not 'home' with Christ yet.

James may just mean that his readers are the people of God, scattered far from their real home. Later he will ask them to remember 'our father Abraham' (2:21), so perhaps James is writing to converted Jews who had once lived in Jerusalem but have had to move away.

But possibly these opening words convey something more too. '... the twelve tribes scattered' is a phrase that describes God's Old Testament people at a particular time of their history. God scattered these tribes among the nations in judgment at the time of the exile. God did this because of his people's spiritual adultery and sinful behaviour.

We will find that there are a number of similarities between the church James is addressing and Israel back then. James will call these believers spiritual adulterers and he will speak to them about the danger of God's judgment.

It may just be that this phrase is the first note in James' spiritual wake-up call to these believers.

PRAY

Thank God for the privilege of being part of his chosen people. Pray you would be faithful to him.

Can a gap develop between what we know and how we actually behave? Yes. Very easily!

All through his letter James calls on these Christians to act in line with what they say they believe. He begins here with the issue of how they respond to the various trials that come their way. Every trial we face puts our trust in Jesus under pressure. They test our faith. Is our faith real? Will it last?

- *What do these believers already know about the outcome of such tests (v. 3)?*

Experiencing a trial is like going through a testing assault course. Negotiating the course will have many challenges, but if we keep going, we will be stronger and more resilient as a result.

The more we persevere in our faith through trials, the stronger our trust in Jesus will become and the more we *will* keep going. We will learn to persevere whatever happens. Trials can actually help us stay Christian.

All this is not news to James' readers. They know this (v. 3).

But knowing this should not be a fact filed away somewhere gathering dust. It should change how they respond to trials.

- *How should these believers think about having to face trials (v. 2)?*

We must not misunderstand James here. James does not say, 'Feel pure joy ... whenever you face trials.' James is not talking here about trying to feel something. He is talking about deciding to think something. The word 'consider' in verse 2 carries the idea of counting or reckoning. It means deliberately deciding to think in a certain way.

Imagine you are writing down all the experiences of your life. There are two columns on the piece of paper, one headed 'Joy' and the other headed 'Difficult'. You have to decide where to record each experience. As you think about each one, you have to decide, 'Should this experience go in the "Joy" column? Or should I put it down in the other column?'

James is saying that, in their thinking, believers need to put trials down in the 'Joy' column. And they need to *keep* putting trials back into the 'Joy' column in their minds, for it is very easy to stray from thinking like this. We should do this, not because these trials *feel* joyful at the time, for they probably won't, but because these testing times can help us stay Christian. James will go on to tell his readers why staying Christian is so very important.

PRAY

Pray that the testing of your faith would produce perseverance.

We love a quick fix, especially one that is easy and trouble-free.

But sometimes a project takes a long time to complete and much patience is needed. In today's verse, James calls on his readers to have just this sort of patience.

James has had some striking things to say about trials. He has been reminding his readers that testing makes our faith in Christ more resilient. Trusting Christ through trial after trial helps us keep going right to the end. Such testing will help us reach the finishing line, but that is not all. As we persevere through trials, we will also be transformed in the process.

Trials produce perseverance and James pictures this perseverance as a worker with a job to finish. The job is a long-term project and progress may appear very slow. Patience will be needed. But we need to keep faith with this 'worker' and not reject them; we mustn't go looking around for an alternative one to do the job.

• *If we do 'let perseverance finish its work', what will be the result (v. 4)?*

When we are in the midst of trials, our spiritual life and our godliness can seem pretty ragged. We can feel as if we are only just clinging on to faith in God by our fingertips. Trials can show up all sorts of weaknesses and sins in our lives that need sorting.

We may not feel as if we are becoming 'mature and complete, not lacking anything', as James promises here. It is very tempting to look for other routes to spiritual maturity and godly character, especially if they look quick and trouble-free.

But James calls on his Christian readers to 'let perseverance finish its work'. They are to trust that, in the end, this process of persevering faithfully through trials will complete its job of changing them for the better.

In testing times everything can seem out of control. We just don't know what is coming down the line, at least that is how it seems. James wants to reassure these believers, because what is coming for them is transformation. In the end, they will be a finished work of great beauty and worth! James wants his friends to stand back from the challenges of today and look on to the end – that will help them to persevere and help them keep counting trials as 'pure joy'.

PRAY

Thank God that as we persevere through trials, we will become 'mature and complete', lacking nothing. Ask him to help you believe that.

In testing times, it can be very hard to know what to do for the best.

• *What should we do if we feel we lack wisdom? What encouragements does James give (v. 5)?*

Wisdom in the Bible has nothing to do with exam grades or brilliant brains. Biblical wisdom means knowing how to please God and obey his word in any situation, however challenging it may be.

James' reassuring message is that God will give us the wisdom we need to get through every trial. We just need to ask! God will help us know how to put his word into practice in our particular circumstances.

And God is not stingy or reluctant. Our God 'gives generously to all without finding fault' (v. 5). Because of Jesus, God does not treat us as our sins deserve; in his mercy and grace, God gives his wisdom to every believer who seriously seeks it.

Some people though say prayers asking for wisdom but don't end up wise at all. The problem here is not with God's giving but with their receiving. If you say a prayer asking for wisdom but end up foolish, you can be sure that the problem is never on God's side.

Perhaps you have had the experience of talking to someone who doesn't hear your words because they are listening intently to something else. James seems to be describing a similar situation in verses 6–8. Here is someone who doesn't end up with wisdom, even though God is very willing to give it.

• *What kind of person 'should not expect to receive anything from the Lord' (vv. 6–8)?*

This is not talking about the doubts of honest questions. No, James is describing here someone who is trying to go in two directions at once. This person is trying to combine worshipping God with worshipping something else. They are 'double-minded' (v. 8) – doubtful about whether they will obey God or not. Spiritually speaking, they have their ears plugged with earphones that are not tuned in to the 'channel' of God's wisdom. They are giving their attention to other voices. 'Wisdom' may be included on their prayer list but they aren't that serious about receiving it. And so they don't.

The way such people respond to testing times will be totally unreliable. They are like tossing waves, 'unstable in all they do' (v. 8). Will they go God's way or not? Who knows?

If we want God's wisdom to help us in our trials, we must seek it with an undivided heart.

PRAY

Ask God to give you wisdom to help you know how to persevere and please him through the trials you face.

What will God's wisdom look like? Today's verses are like a worked example of how to be wise and it is one that seems very close to home for James' readers. The example James picks is how to respond to wealth, or the lack of it. These believers need this wisdom if they are going to persevere faithfully and grow in godliness in the process.

• *How should 'believers in humble circumstances' respond to being near the bottom of the heap financially (v. 9)?*

This sounds very odd. These Christians don't appear to have a high position at all, humanly speaking. But as we read on, James will remind his readers, 'has not God chosen those who are poor in the eyes of the world to be rich in faith and to inherit the kingdom he promised those who love him?' (2:5).

No one is choosing these believers for well-paid jobs now, but God has chosen them to be spiritually wealthy for all eternity. They need to hold their heads up and take pride in being among God's chosen ones – there is no higher position. Here is a word for us too, if we are in humble circumstances.

• *What is the rich person like and why? What should he or she 'take pride in' (vv. 10–11)?*

Wild flowers are beautiful, but only very briefly. In the heat of the midday sun, they and their splendour are quickly destroyed. The rich are just like that; they look glorious now, but their lives and their glory can be gone without warning in a moment. They can't control the future; their lives are fragile and finite, and they need to remember that! This truth needs to be 'centre stage' in how the rich think about themselves. They need to 'take pride' in it (v. 10)! Thinking like this will help them stay humble and that is the only safe place to be spiritually.

James doesn't call these rich people 'believers'. It may be that he is not sure they are. Some of the rich people James has in mind in this letter are clearly not behaving like believers and he will call on them to repent. Whether they do will show whether they are real believers or not.

We may not think of our financial situation as a test of our faith, but in a way it is. We need to see ourselves and our situation from God's point of view and in the light of eternity. That is true wisdom.

 **DAY 7**

A re you a blessed person? Is God's favour resting on you?

You may look at your current circumstances and not feel very blessed at all.

James has begun his letter by speaking to his Christian friends about testing times. He expects them to face trials of many kinds. Being a Christian is no guarantee of an easy life, quite the reverse actually. You may look at your experience of life now and not be able to see much evidence that God's favour is resting on you.

- *But what is the right way to spot a blessed person, according to James (v. 12)?*

You can't tell who is blessed by looking at how easy or hard a person's life seems to be now. The thing to look for is their perseverance. Has this person kept on trusting and loving Christ through every trial that has come their way? Have they 'stood the test', or have they given up on their faith? James is very clear here: 'Blessed is the one who perseveres under trial'. That is how you tell if someone has God's blessing. Look for the person who is keeping on keeping on!

- *Why is this person blessed (v. 12)?*

This person is blessed because of what is awaiting them in the future. James wants to lift the gaze of his brothers and sisters from the trials of today to what is coming. Testing times won't last forever. In the end, the person who stands the test and perseveres in loving the Lord Jesus will receive 'the crown of life'. That is what he has promised us.

Being a Christian now is an experience of both loving and trusting. We love the Lord Jesus and we trust his promises. In the gospel, the Lord promises to give eternal life to those who love him, and we can be certain that he will do what he has said. You may be in humble or difficult circumstances now, but you have a glorious future coming.

No wonder James told his friends, 'Consider it pure joy ... whenever you face trials of many kinds' (1:2). It is these tests of faith that produce perseverance in us. This testing develops our patience and steadfastness so that we do keep going.

Persevering in trusting and loving Jesus is really important. For it is the one who perseveres to the end who is blessed, and no one else.

PRAY

Thank God for his promise to give the crown of life to those who persevere in loving and trusting him. Ask him to help you do that, whatever happens.

Every believer is tempted to sin, especially in trying times. You will know that first-hand. Some sinful thought or word or action can seem very attractive, even though you know it is wrong.

- *Why are we tempted? What is the wrong answer to this question and why (v. 13)?*

God never pulled anyone in the direction of doing wrong. He is not responsible in any way for drawing us towards sin.

But perhaps James' readers were looking for excuses for their sinful behaviour. Maybe they were saying, 'God tempted me to do wrong. God has put me in this difficult trial so it's no wonder I am behaving like this! That makes God partly responsible for my sin, doesn't it?!'

When we sin, we like to point the finger away from ourselves. We look for someone or something to blame. But James points the finger firmly in the opposite direction.

- *What is the right answer to why we are tempted (v. 14)?*

James points to our hearts. We feel tempted to sin when we are pulled towards it by our own desires. We sin because doing or saying or thinking something wrong is attractive to us in some way. We want to do it.

This is very searching.

Imagine a table spread with all kinds of foods – chocolate, beetroot, crisps, liver, ice cream, strawberries, squid – every kind of food you can picture. Which foods would you find most 'tempting'? Which foods could you pass by pretty easily or maybe not find tempting at all? It all depends on what you like. The more you like it, the more tempting it will be for you. What we find most tempting will be different for each of us, but whatever it is, it reveals our desires. It uncovers what we want.

It is just like that with sin. We sin because we want to. Testing situations are the occasion not the cause of our sin; the cause is our own sinful desires. That is exactly why 'God cannot be tempted by evil' (v. 13) for God has no evil desires in his heart at all. We, however, have lots and that is why we find all sorts of sins attractive. We desire what we think sinful behaviour will bring us; that may be pleasure or wealth or status or perhaps just a sense of superiority over others.

As with favourite foods, which sins seem most tempting will be different for different people. Someone who hates the taste of alcohol may not find drunkenness much of a temptation. That person though may find slanderous gossip very attractive. Examine the sins you find most tempting. It will show you a lot about your heart.

PRAY

Ask God to help you examine the desires of your own heart and to turn from evil ones.

 **DAY 9**

It is very dangerous to follow all the desires of our hearts. We love the Lord and want to please him, but we have lots of sinful desires too. Our hearts can easily be divided, so we need to watch out!

There is a sinister and dangerous force on the loose, beckoning and pressuring us towards sin. The culprit is not God or the circumstances he allows us to experience. Temptation comes from our 'own evil desire' (v. 14); it comes from within our own hearts. When we give in to temptation, there can be no excuses; we have no one to blame but ourselves.

• *James uses very graphic language to describe what is happening. How does he describe what our evil desires do (v. 14)?*

James makes our sinful desires sound like a clever and dangerous kidnapper. These desires tempt us, whispering subtle and attractive lies that sound so plausible: 'It would be perfectly understandable to behave like that, under the circumstances' ... 'It will make you feel better' ... 'It will do you good.' Lies. All lies. We are enticed and pulled towards sin by the selfish desires that constantly well up in our own hearts.

Does it really matter that much if we obey these inner whispers? What will happen if we do? Many times in this letter James points his readers to the consequences of today's decisions. He does so here.

• *Persevering in loving and trusting Christ will lead to receiving the crown of life in the end (1:12). But what will the habit of giving in to temptation lead to? (v. 15)?*

Here is an ugly family tree. Nurture the flicker of an evil thought and you will soon find that a sinful action or attitude has sprouted into life and is growing stronger every day. Sin breeds. It spreads. An action becomes a habit, and a habit becomes a character and a way of life. The end result will be death: separation from God forever.

You may be thinking, 'Surely, when I do something wrong, I can repent and ask Christ for his forgiveness?' Yes, you can. And wonderfully, Christ freely forgives those who sincerely repent and seek his grace. But James' double-minded readers need a serious warning against taking sin lightly. James' message is do not settle down with your sin. Do not let it become 'full-grown'. Cut it down before disobeying God becomes the whole direction of your life. Be killing sin before it is killing you! Don't be deceived: the root of sin is in your heart, in your desires. Be very careful what you wish for.

PRAY

Pray you would heed James' warning too.

How do you think about God? James clearly thinks his readers are in danger of being deceived (v. 16). They need to wise up about their sin and about God too. The source of our sin is never God, so we can't shift any blame to him. The consequence of leaving sin unchecked will be spiritual death. We must not let sin flourish and become 'full-grown' (1:15). We must persevere in killing it off.

Now James will remind his readers of what God's gifts are really like. This will underline how wrong it is to think that God would ever 'give' someone a temptation!

• **What do we learn here about God and his gifts (v. 17)?**

God is so different from us. In our double-mindedness we can often be like 'a wave ... blown and tossed by the wind' (1:6). Our responses can be so unreliable.

But God is always the same. He 'does not change like shifting shadows'. He always gives good gifts and always has done. He gave the whole universe life, 'fathering' the 'heavenly lights'. He has always been on the side of light, not of darkness and deception.

• **What special good gift has God given to believers? How and why did he give it (v. 18)?**

What a contrast to those ugly 'births' of sin and death, products of our own evil desires (1:15)! God has chosen to give believers a very different sort of birth.

God has brought us to life spiritually and he has done it 'through the word of truth'. As we heard and responded to the gospel message about Jesus, our new lives began. God's word is very powerful. God spoke and the universe was born. His word has brought us to spiritual birth too.

God has desires in his heart but, unlike ours, his desires and plans are always good. His gift of new birth is a gift with a purpose. He wants believers to be 'a kind of firstfruits of all he created'. This is an image from Old Testament days. The firstfruits of any farm crop were set apart to belong to God in a special way.

That is God's desire for us. Out of all that he has created, God wants us to be specially his own.

Picking the 'firstfruits' was also a sign that the harvest was beginning. Receiving the seed of God's word is to be only the beginning too. God is looking for a great harvest of righteousness in us!

PRAY

Thank God for all the good gifts he has given you, especially the gift of spiritual birth.

It matters a great deal how we respond to God's word.

God gives us birth spiritually through his 'word of truth' (1:18) as we hear the gospel of Jesus and turn from our sin. But we must also keep responding to God's word in the right way. James pictures God's word as a seed that God has 'planted' in believers. God wants this 'seed' to be productive; he is looking for a harvest.

- *How must we respond to the word God has 'planted' in us and why (v. 21b)?*

Hearing God's word is not always a comfortable experience. When our wrongdoing is exposed, it is easy to snap straight back with angry excuses or denials. We don't usually like being told we need to change. Yet we must humbly accept what God says about us. It is vital that we do so, for this word can save us. Hearing and responding rightly to God's word is the means God uses to keep us safe spiritually.

James tells us what humbly accepting God's word will look like in practice. This is how he wants his readers to respond to the challenging words of his letter.

- *What are James' dos and don'ts for responding to God's word (vv. 19–21a)?*

It seems likely that James is thinking here about how we respond to God's word to us about our sin. This is the word that we are probably least keen to listen to and the word which is most likely to make us angry or provoke us to immediately answer back with arguments or excuses.

Instead we must respond to this word by taking drastic action to 'get rid of all moral filth and the evil that is so prevalent' (v. 21) and to start producing 'the righteousness that God desires' (v. 20). We need to take our sin as seriously as God does. James is concerned about his readers' attitude to their sin. He has already warned them that if they let sin become 'full-grown', it 'gives birth to death' (1:15).

How we respond to God's word is how we respond to God. It is a litmus test of our spiritual safety. If we start rejecting or ignoring God's calls to change, we are in a very dangerous place. When God speaks, we are to be quick to listen, slow to answer back and slow to get angry. We are to humbly accept his word. God has planted his word in us and he wants it to produce righteousness! How are you listening?

PRAY

Ask God to help you humbly accept his word.

God's word can save us! Failing to listen to his word and failing to accept it is very dangerous.

But there is another danger James is concerned about too. This danger is sneaky and easily missed. It is a very effective scam.

• *How does James describe this deception (vv. 22–24)?*

Dangerous false teachers have always found their way into churches. But actually all believers have a false teacher resident in their own heads. We deceive ourselves; we tell ourselves lies. One of our most effective deceptions can happen after we listen to God's word. We nod in agreement as we hear what God says and this humble nodding makes us feel that we are making great progress spiritually. We can easily overlook the fact that a week later absolutely nothing in our life has changed. We resolve to obey God's word but these good intentions never turn into action.

James uses the brilliant illustration of looking in a mirror to help his readers see this danger. Mirrors show us what we look like. They are also agents of change, for they show us what we need to do. You might look in a mirror and see that you have dirt on your face. You should go away and wash! But if you forget what you look like and stay dirty, looking in the mirror does you no good

at all. It is just like that if we hear God's call to change, accept that we need to change, but then fail to take action.

• *How should we respond to God's word and what can God's word bring us (v. 25)?*

Some kinds of listening are more helpful than others. If you only have a brief cursory glance in a mirror once a week, you are not likely to take good care of your appearance. We need to look much more carefully and regularly! How much more should we gaze into the mirror of God's word, his 'perfect law', both intently and continually.

How we hear God's word makes a big difference to our obedience to it, and it is obedience that matters. In Jesus' famous parable of the sower (Luke 8:4–15), every person hears God's word, but it is only the one who keeps obeying it who is fruitful.

God's commands are not a cage designed to lock us away from good things. Living life in obedience to our maker's instructions is actually the only way to true freedom and blessing (v. 25). God want to do us good!

PRAY

Pray you would look intently and continually into God's word and then take action to obey it.

How do you think your spiritual life is going?

It seems that our own assessment may not always be correct. Once again, we may be deceiving ourselves. The 'false teacher' who lives in our heads and feeds us lies keeps very busy!

We may have a tendency to give ourselves a good 'write-up' as we reflect on our spiritual lives. We may remember our regular visits to church and feel rather pleased with ourselves.

- *But what really shows if our claim to be 'religious' is worth anything (vv. 26–27)?*

James mentions three aspects of believers' lives here. He wants his readers to inspect how they are doing in these areas. This will give them a much more accurate assessment of their spiritual health than just checking how many religious meetings they attend.

James will return to each issue later in his letter. This list is like an agenda of his concerns.

The first issue James points to is self-control, and in particular whether we can control our tongues. Words are tremendously powerful. God's words brought physical life to the universe and spiritual life to us. Our words have power too. They can bring truth and love and peace. They can build good relationships. Or they can be false and hateful and destructive. James will have a lot more to say about taming the tongue (3:1–12), but his big point is clear: don't think your spiritual life is going well if your words are out of control.

The second issue James highlights is how we treat those who are most vulnerable and needy. Orphans and widows in James' society often had no one to provide for them. This again is a very practical test of the reality of our faith, for caring for the needy is demanding; it is likely to demand our money, our time and our effort.

The third issue is holiness. The sinful attitudes of those around us can rub off on us. James wants his readers 'to keep' themselves 'from being polluted by the world' (v. 27). This too is an issue of self-control; it won't 'just happen'.

- *How does James describe God (v. 27)?*

If we believe in Jesus, we are *already* in God's family, for God is our Father. But his grace should not make us complacent. God wants us to grow like him. He cares a great deal if there is a credibility gap between our claim to be his children and our actual behaviour.

PRAY

Ask God to help you see where there are gaps between your beliefs and your behaviour.

How will you treat other people today?

James' readers are busy doing religious things. They are meeting together, hearing God's word and talking about God. They clearly consider themselves religious.

But as we read on in James' letter, it seems that personal relationships in this church are in a terrible state. We will hear of fights, quarrels, snobbery, sneering, discrimination, hatred, lies, slander, bragging, boasting and a failure to help those in need.

Our relationships with people reveal a great deal about how we are actually relating to God. No wonder James is concerned.

There are clearly glaring gaps between the faith these believers profess and their behaviour. James wants to wake these believers up to the danger they are in.

James imagines a very telling incident. Perhaps it isn't entirely imaginary. In this story, before the church meeting has even begun, the Christians attending have already failed all three of James' tell-tale tests of genuine religion (1:26–27). They have been 'polluted by the world', not cared for the vulnerable and spoken some shocking words!

• *What happens in this imaginary incident and what does it show?*

Isn't this just how the unbelieving world treats people? The worldly glory of wealth and status is obvious. It impresses. Unbelievers will often treat rich people differently, for if we favour the rich, they may return the favour.

Poor people though have nothing to give in return for favours. They have little power to complain when treated badly and so, sadly, they often are.

How terrible if the church mirrors the world in the way it behaves towards rich and poor.

If James' readers show such favouritism, they have 'discriminated' among themselves and 'become judges with evil thoughts' (v. 4). Such behaviour reveals what is going on in their hearts. Proud and evil motivations are uncovered in this judgmental behaviour. Such divisions in the fellowship are evidence again of these believers' divided hearts.

• *How does James describe his readers (v. 1)?*

James reminds them of who they are so that they see the shocking mismatch with their behaviour. They are James' 'brothers and sisters' and so they are 'believers in our glorious Lord Jesus Christ'.

The 'glory' of earthly riches will soon be gone; only the Lord Jesus has real and lasting glory.

Now he is the risen and glorified Lord, but on earth Jesus was poor. He might well have been told to 'sit on the floor' by these Christians. What a shock that is.

And Jesus, their Lord, welcomed rich and poor alike. Showing favouritism couldn't be more out of place among Jesus' people.

PRAY

Pray that your church family would welcome all people in the way God has welcomed us.

Is treating rich and poor differently really such a big deal?

James clearly thinks that it is. Showing favouritism just doesn't fit with being in God's family, for God does not give rich people preferential treatment. He gives his grace freely to anyone who believes in Jesus.

• *What is the difference between how God relates to the poor and how James' readers do (vv. 5–6a)?*

God is not impressed by human wealth. He doesn't check people's bank balances before deciding who to welcome into his family. James wants his dear brothers and sisters to look around their church and see that this is true. There are believers in their fellowship who don't have much money. Those Christians may not have been chosen for jobs with big salaries, but God has chosen them to be 'rich in faith' (v. 5). This is the kind of wealth that really matters, for those who love God will inherit his kingdom. That is God's promise and he is trustworthy. Believers may be poor now, but they have vast wealth coming their way in the age to come. God will treat them very well indeed.

James' readers on the other hand have 'dishonoured the poor'. What a contrast! They are behaving just like the unbelieving world and not at all like their Father in heaven.

• *What does James say about how the rich are relating to Christ and his people (vv. 6b–7)?*

These believers have been looking down on the poor for not having much money and they have totally missed the real issue. What matters is not your relationship with your bank but your relationship with God. Again, James wants his readers to look around. They have been honouring the wrong people. The rich people they honour are blaspheming Christ's name and persecuting Christ's people. It is perfectly obvious that these people are God's enemies. There is nothing honourable to say about them!

James is clearly writing to a specific situation. Not all rich people drag Christians into court and not all poor people are 'rich in faith'. But there are still very important lessons here. We need to flip on its head the way the world judges people.

What matters is whether people love Jesus or oppose him. Many poor people love Jesus; God chooses them and honours them by giving them his kingdom. Will we honour them in the way our Father does?

PRAY

Ask God to help you honour those the world despises.

'Love your neighbour as yourself' (Lev. 19:18).

King Jesus quoted this Old Testament command and so James calls it here 'the royal law'. Jesus taught that this command summed up all God's laws about how we should treat one other (Matt. 22:37–39), for of course, if you love your neighbour you will not take his life or his wife.

It may be that James' religious readers thought they were doing well at keeping this law. After all, they probably weren't guilty of murdering anyone or committing adultery. But James wants these Christians to see that they are deceiving themselves. They are not keeping this 'royal law' as they should and this is serious. Loving your neighbour isn't just about avoiding lying, stealing, murder and adultery.

• *How else might someone be breaking this law (v. 9)?*

James' message is that when you treat rich and poor differently and favour the rich, the law declares you to be a law-breaker. So, if you show favouritism, don't think you are doing fine in your Christian life, for you are a spiritual criminal! When you judge others, you are failing to love them as Jesus commands. His law convicts you and finds you guilty. Judge others and you will find yourself judged!

James' readers might think this verdict is a bit harsh. After all, there are probably lots of God's laws they haven't broken.

• *How does James explain why the law's verdict on favouritism is so serious (vv. 10–11)?*

When we open our Bibles, we find lots of different laws. But James talks here about 'the whole law', as if there is actually just one big law. It seems that there is a unity to God's law which means that breaking it anywhere breaks the whole of it.

The unity of God's law flows from the unity of God himself. Yes, there are individual commands, but these are not like separate, unconnected items on a list. Each one is spoken by the same God and together they reflect the whole picture of his character. So there is a 'whole law' which is shattered like a pane of mirror glass when any individual command is broken.

James' readers may have thought that how they treated rich and poor didn't matter much. But James wants his readers to see that showing favouritism breaks the 'royal' summary law (v. 8): to love one's neighbour. We cannot just pick some of the ways God wants us to love and dismiss others. Favouritism, adultery and murder all break God's law of love, and being guilty of any one of these commands makes us a law-breaker. How we treat each other in seemingly small matters is not a small matter to God.

PRAY

Ask God to help you see the ways you fail to love your neighbour as yourself and to see again how much you need his mercy and forgiveness.

How should the gospel change the way you relate to people?

James wants to wake his readers up. He wants them to see how serious it is to treat the poor in their congregation differently from the rich. This behaviour doesn't fit with how believers in the glorious Lord Jesus Christ should behave. It is not how God behaves towards the poor and it breaks God's law which commands us to love our neighbours as ourselves.

We have no right to behave like judges over people, honouring some and dishonouring others.

• *How should we behave instead (v. 12)?*

Rather than behaving like judges, we are to live as people who will be judged ourselves. Our lives are going to be compared with God's law – that reflection of his perfect character – to see how well they measure up.

Jesus once said, 'Be merciful, just as your Father is merciful' (Luke 6:36). Christians have received mercy from God in the gospel. Now we are to behave like our heavenly Father and treat others with mercy too.

• *What will happen to those who don't treat others with mercy (v. 13)?*

Measured against God's law of love, all of us will be found to be law-breakers. How much we need judgment with mercy! But we should not expect God to be merciful to us if we have withheld mercy from those around us. For Jesus went on to say, '… with the measure you use, it will be measured to you' (Luke 6:38). This is a serious warning.

James knows that his readers have not been honouring the poor or treating them with grace. They have not showered the poor with blessings they do not deserve and could never repay – quite the opposite in fact: they have not been merciful to them at all.

James' point is that if you have really received God's mercy, your behaviour will change. You will want to keep God's law and become like him. Keeping his law still matters and keeping his law is also good for us. This law 'gives freedom', for loving our neighbour turns us outwards from the slavery of our self-centredness. The gospel of grace frees us to love like God loves.

How we live matters. Believers are to live as those whose lives are to be measured against God's perfect law. Of course, if that was the end of the story, we would always be condemned. But praise God that judgment will not be the last word for true believers, for mercy 'triumphs' over judgment (v. 13). And that should be the pattern in our relationships with one another too.

PRAY

Ask God to help you speak and act today with mercy towards others, especially those who cannot repay you in any way.

Mind the gap! God does not change like shifting shadows. There is a reliability and a consistency and a unity about everything he says and does. But the life of a double-minded Christian is very different. It is full of gaps and inconsistencies.

We may listen to God's word but never put it into practice. We may consider ourselves religious, but our lives may tell a different story. Jesus our Lord gives grace and mercy to the poor, but we may fail to do the same.

James' readers are failing in exactly these ways and James wants them to see the danger they are in. Gaps matter, and in today's verses James shines his spotlight on yet another one.

• **What important question does James raise (v. 14)?**

The gap James highlights here is between what we say and what we do. Is it possible to claim to believe in Jesus but not be saved? Is there such a thing as fake or counterfeit 'faith' which will turn out to be useless?

• **Where is the gap in the story that James uses to illustrate his answer (vv. 15–16)?**

James still seems to be thinking about how his readers treat poor Christians in their fellowship. He imagines a very shocking incident to demonstrate his point.

He paints a picture of a Christian brother or sister who is destitute. They have no clothes and nothing to eat. It is no good wishing this poor believer warmth and food if you give them neither. Such good wishes are hollow and fake. If you really wished your brother or sister well, you wouldn't leave them cold and hungry.

The way you tell that such good wishes are genuine is that they turn into action. The evidence that you mean what you say is that you actually do it. Words don't fill hungry stomachs; you need to give your brother or sister practical help, otherwise your claim to care is useless.

Claims to have faith are just as useless if there is no evidence in your actions that you believe what you say. James says such 'faith' is dead (v. 17). In other words, James' answer to the question he raised in verse 14 is 'no'.

Claims to believe in the Lord Jesus that don't lead to obedient action are fake claims. They will do us no good at all. Such 'faith' will not save us.

PRAY

Ask God to help you see where there are similar gaps in your Christian life and ask for his forgiveness and power to change.

How do you respond when your behaviour is challenged? It is always tempting to look for excuses.

James' words have been very challenging. Not everyone who claims to have faith in Jesus will be saved. Faith that does not lead to action is not authentic faith at all. James calls it 'dead' (2:17). It is good for nothing!

James' readers claim to believe in Jesus. How will they respond to this very serious warning? Repentance would have been good, but it seems that James expects an argument.

'You have faith; I have deeds,' says James' imaginary speaker (v. 18), as if faith and deeds were a pair of matching and optional spiritual gifts. No need for me to have both, is there? That seems to be the gist of this speaker's argument.

• **Which of the pair is this imaginary speaker claiming to have (v. 18)?**

James is being provocative. It is actually far more likely that James' lazy readers would have said the sentence the other way round, for their problem was that they *didn't* have deeds. Arguing, 'I have faith, you have deeds' would have been a convenient way to brush aside James' call for action!

But they can't brush his warning away like this. If they have faith and no deeds, their faith is useless. James sets up a challenge to drive his point home.

• **What challenge does James give his readers (v. 18)?**

There is no way that his readers can do what James asks. A 'faith without deeds' has nothing to see, so you can't *show* it to anyone. No one can see another person's heart.

James can demonstrate his faith is genuine though. 'I will show you my faith', he says, 'by my deeds.' That is how you tell what someone really believes inside – take a good look at what they do!

All genuine faith in the Lord Jesus leads to obedient action. Every true believer will have both faith and deeds.

James' readers cannot wriggle off the hook and excuse their poor behaviour. 'Faith' without action really is 'dead' and useless. It will save no one.

• **Who has this sort of 'dead', useless 'faith'? Are they expecting their 'faith' to save them (v. 19)?**

This is another shocking illustration. Demons are God's enemies. They know there is only one God but they do not obey him. Will their belief save them? Absolutely not! In fact, demons shudder when they think about God. They know he will judge and destroy them.

Believing there is one God is good. But if you don't obey him, you are in no better position than demons. Your 'faith' won't save you, for it isn't genuine faith at all.

PRAY

Ask God to help you see where you are making excuses for not obeying him as you should.

How foolish it is to think that all is well between you and God if you are refusing to obey him!

James is warning his complacent readers. He gives them evidence that faith without obedient deeds is 'useless' (v. 20) by looking at the importance of action in Abraham's life.

• *Why was Abraham 'considered right-eous' (v. 21)?*

James is picking up on the incident in Abraham's life recorded in Genesis 22. There, Abraham obeys God's command and puts his son, Isaac, on an altar. God spares Isaac and then tells Abraham that he will bless him in extraordinary ways 'because you have obeyed me' (Gen. 22:18).

Is this salvation by works? No. 'Righteousness' had already been 'credited' to Abraham many years before this, just because he trusted God (v. 23). In verse 23, James quotes this earlier incident recorded in Genesis 15:6. There is no mention of Abraham *doing* anything at all at that earlier time. Abraham became 'God's friend' just because he trusted him.

• *So what was the relationship between Abraham's faith and his later obedience (vv. 22–23)?*

As Abraham lifted his precious son onto that altar, his faith and his actions 'were working together' (v. 22). Abraham's inner trust in God was flowing out into active obedience. What he did was really just a demonstration of his faith in God – that is why he was 'considered righteous' for what he did (v. 21).

This later obedience made Abraham's faith 'complete' (v. 22). It 'fulfilled' that earlier scripture about Abraham believing God (v. 23).

In what way was Abraham's faith incomplete until he put his trust in God into practice? Think of it like this: when you fill in a form, there is usually a space at the end for your signature. You sign there to confirm that everything you have written above it is true. Signing the form doesn't make it true, but it makes a clear declaration that it is. If you don't sign, the form is incomplete.

Obeying God is a bit like signing your claim to trust him. It confirms that you really do. In this sense, Abraham's actions 'completed' his faith. His earlier promise to trust God was 'fulfilled'.

Look along a true believer's timeline and you will see that trusting God is always followed by doing what God says. Genuine faith will always show itself in obedience.

James' message in verse 24 is stark and challenging. If you claim to trust God but then refuse to obey him, don't think God will accept you.

PRAY

Give thanks that, because of Christ's death, our faith is 'credited to [us] as righteousness'. Pray you would express this trust in your obedience to him.

It doesn't matter who you are, this challenge applies to you!

James has been warning his complacent and disobedient readers. It is possible to claim to believe and yet not be saved (2:14–17). Real faith always shows itself in obedient action. Look at the example of Abraham, that great father of the Jewish nation!

Now James points to another Old Testament believer, Rahab. Unlike Abraham, Rahab wasn't Jewish or respectable. She was working as a prostitute when she heard about the one true God.

• *Why was Rahab 'considered righteous' (v. 25)?*

Abraham had personal encounters with God but Rahab only heard second-hand reports about him (Josh. 2:8–13). Yet Rahab clearly came to believe in God. How do we know? Her faith was revealed in what she did.

Joshua sent spies to survey the promised land and Rahab helped these representatives of God's people. Doing so was risky and dangerous; she put her life on the line for God. The Old Testament account doesn't mention Rahab's faith specifically, but her outward behaviour showed what was going on in her heart. Abraham and Rahab were different in many ways but they both put their trust in God into action; you could see what they believed in what they did.

James' message to his disobedient readers is clear. Whoever you are, whatever your background, real saving faith *always* shows itself in obedient action. That was true long ago and it is still true today. James' readers must not think they can wriggle out of this challenge, and nor must we!

James takes his readers to the graphic image of a dead body to drive his point home one last time. Think of a physical body. Without living breath, without a spirit, all you have before you is a useless corpse.

• *In James' illustration, is it faith or deeds which is like a body (v. 26)?*

This is unexpected. After all, deeds, like a physical body, can be seen and heard, whereas inner faith, like a spirit, cannot.

James surprises us here. He says that it is 'faith' that is like a physical body, for, like a physical body, his readers' loud claims to faith are easy to spot. But if a body has the spirit of life in it, you will see it moving. If it is completely motionless, you can be sure it is dead. In the same way, a faith that is 'alive' will 'move'; it will take action to obey God.

James' point is this: just as a body without a spirit is dead, in the same way 'faith' which is not accompanied by obedient actions is dead too.

PRAY

Pray you would heed James' warning and that your own faith would be visible in what you do.

What should you look for in teachers of God's word?

God's word is very powerful. God gives believers birth spiritually 'through the word of truth' (1:18). Now James is calling his wayward readers back to 'humbly accept the word planted in [them], which can save [them]' (1:21). This word comes to the congregation through teachers. So what James says next is, at first sight, very surprising.

- **How many people in this congregation should become teachers (v. 1)?**

This is a shock. You might think this dysfunctional community of Christians needs as many teachers of God's word as they can get!

- **Why is it that not many in this wayward congregation should become teachers (v. 1)?**

Teachers have great power to help or harm God's people. Their words are heard not just by one or two individuals but by everyone. And their example will be followed, for good or ill. No wonder James says that 'we who teach will be judged more strictly'.

To be a teacher of God's word you need, according to the New Testament, to teach in two ways – lip and life. You need to teach the truth with your lips, but you also need to model that truth in how you live.

The Christians James is writing to don't seem to be 'walking the talk', so few of them are fit to be teachers. There are gaps and inconsistencies everywhere! They claim to have faith but obedient deeds are sorely lacking. The way they are treating each other is very different from how God in his mercy has treated them. These double-minded believers are pursuing pleasure rather than godliness, and loving the world more than God (4:1–4).

James' readers may need some convincing of the truth of his shocking assessment of them. So James goes on to talk to them about talking. Teachers of course are usually very gifted at talking, but being good at communication skills is not enough to be a teacher of God's word.

Our words reveal so much about us, as James will go on to show. What he has to say will humble his readers and it should humble us too. Perhaps many of James' readers were keen to set themselves up as teachers in the congregation. But if you want to know how suitable you are to talk about God in this way, look at how you talk about everyone else!

PRAY

Pray for the teachers in your own congregation, that they would live out the truth they teach.

How conscious are you of your sin? It seems that James' complacent readers are in danger of deceiving themselves about theirs. James has told this dysfunctional congregation that not many of them should be teachers of God's word. Teachers need to model the gospel they explain. James' readers claim to have faith, but their lives tell a different story – that is why so few of them fit the bill.

Of course, no teacher is a perfect illustration of godliness though.

• *What does James say is true of everyone, even teachers (v. 2)?*

Unlike his readers, James is humble. He himself is a teacher, but he is not claiming to be perfect. He knows that all of us stumble in a whole variety of ways. We just can't stop doing wrong, and you can see that, perhaps most clearly of all, by looking at what we say.

• *What does James say about the person who is never at fault in what he says (v. 2)?*

Self-control is a very big deal in the Christian life. With God's help, we are called to take ourselves in hand and to stop doing wrong and start doing right. James says that the day we master the words that come out of our mouths is the day we will reach perfection.

James' stress on the significance of our words echoes the teaching of Jesus himself. Jesus taught that our words show what is going on in our hearts: 'For out of the overflow of [a person's] heart his mouth speaks' (Luke 6:45).[1]

That is why controlling our words is such a problem. We can't stop saying what we shouldn't because we can't stop wanting what we shouldn't. Our words are just a mirror of our hearts.

In the coming verses James talks about the tongue as if it is a kind of independent being, a sort of wild animal living in our mouths. Actually, of course, the words my tongue speaks are just the thoughts of my heart uncovered and with the volume turned up.

As we read on we will find ourselves agreeing with James as he reflects on the tongue. James' aim though is not primarily to call on us to try harder to master our speech. His aim is rather to show his readers, and us, our hearts.

And as we are humbled in this way, we will see once again our desperate need for God's grace. James' aim is to bring his readers back to God once again in the safety of repentance.

PRAY

Ask God to help you remember your own faults and stumblings, and to walk very humbly with him and with others.

[1] 1984 NIV text.

Why can't we stop saying things we regret?

Look around the world. Human beings have great power to control a whole variety of things. We can make horses 'obey us' (v. 3). We can steer large ships 'wherever the pilot wants to go' (v. 4). 'All kinds of animals, birds, reptiles and sea creatures are being tamed and have been tamed by mankind' (v. 7).

• *But what does James say about 'taming' the tongue (v. 8)?*

The sad fact is that we can't stop saying things we shouldn't. Is this really such a big deal though?

James is writing to a church full of quarrelling, slander and boasting (4:1, 11, 16). Perhaps his complacent readers thought their spiritual lives were fine, despite all this going on. James wants to show them that their words are much more significant than they might think.

Small things can have massive effects. They can control the whole of something. A small bit controls a mighty horse and a small rudder a great ship (vv. 3–4). Small things can also wreak great destruction. A tiny spark can set a whole forest ablaze (v. 5).

The tongue is a small part of the body but its effects are massive too. Rather than us controlling it, the tongue actually controls us. It 'sets the whole course' of a person's life (v. 6), and not in a good way!

James pictures the tongue as a spreading fire from hell, a world of evil living within us which 'corrupts' the whole person with terrifyingly destructive effects (v. 6).

The wagging piece of flesh in our mouths has no mind of its own though. Our tongues just form the words that express what we are like inside. When all the thoughts of our hearts spill straight out of our mouths, the effects are catastrophic. Our relationships, indeed our whole lives, are shaped for good or ill by our words. Lives and relationships can be destroyed by a few brief syllables.

• *How does James describe the tongue (v. 8)?*

It is as if we have a sea of poisonous thoughts constantly tossing around within us. Wave after wave of this vile liquid keeps erupting out of our mouths in what we say.

Our words give the world a demonstration of what is going on in our hearts. Taking an honest look at our words will always be a very humbling experience. It will remind us how much we need God's grace.

PRAY

Confess to God the words you regret saying and then rejoice in his forgiveness.

Praise God that he is so reliable and dependable. He 'does not change like shifting shadows' (1:17).

But we are not like that at all – just look at our words.

• *It is not that everything we say is wrong. What is the issue with words that James is concerned about here (v. 10)?*

God is totally united in all he says and does, but we do not share God's consistency. We bless God one minute and curse those made in his image the next (v. 9). When we open our mouths, you can never be sure what sort of words you will get!

James says 'we' here. *We* praise. *We* curse. He is not claiming he is perfect. He knows, 'We all stumble in many ways' (3:2). But James also doesn't want his readers to excuse or settle down with their foul speech. 'My brothers and sisters,' James says emphatically, 'this should not be' (v. 10).

James wants his wayward readers to grasp how strange their mixed speech should seem to them. Jesus taught that our words flow out of our hearts; they reveal who we are on the inside. James gets his readers to think about how the natural world works to help them see this truth. He points them to water flowing out of springs and fruit growing out of plants.

• *What point is James making through these examples (vv. 11–12)?*

There is a consistency in nature. Fig trees produce figs. Vines produce grapes. Fresh springs produce fresh water. Salt springs produce salt water – always. You don't get one thing one minute and something different the next. The inner nature of these things is stable and fixed, so what they produce is not changeable either.

It is as if James is saying, 'And what about *your* inner nature, dear brothers and sisters? What does your cursing alongside your praising show about that?'

James is concerned that his readers are double-minded. Their hearts are divided and this shows in their speech. Actually, it shows in their outward behaviour in lots of shocking ways and so James doesn't want many of them to be teachers.

As you look around a church family for wise people to teach God's word, what should you look for? Wise words about God are vital. But a wise person is also someone you can rely on not to praise

God one minute and slander you the next. Wisdom is shown in a consistency of life and lip; teaching and living must speak the same message. That is the kind of wise person you want teaching you!

'Who is wise and understanding among you?' (v. 13).

As James thought about the state of the Christians he was addressing, he would probably have answered, 'Hardly anyone!' His readers may well have thought they had lots of spiritual wisdom though. They were clearly talking about spiritual things. But just talking about God doesn't make you a wise person.

• *How do you show that you have real wisdom and understanding (v. 13)?*

As with a tree, you recognise a wise person by the 'fruit' they produce. The wise person is always a humble person. When we humble ourselves before God as we should, we will be humble with others too. We will put their needs above our own selfish desires. True wisdom will always lead to a good life full of good deeds (v. 13).

James contrasts this true wisdom with fake 'wisdom'. It may be that James is describing here exactly what his quarrelling readers were saying and doing. They may have recognised themselves and squirmed as they read on.

James speaks of a situation where people have settled down with their sin. Their hearts are harbouring selfish ambition and bitter envy (v. 14). And rather than being ashamed and repentant, these people are displaying their arrogant selfishness in their words. Their lives contradict the gospel of grace they proclaim. James wants this to stop. If your hearts have gone astray, he says, 'do not boast about it or deny the truth' (v. 14). Don't pass on your spiritual mess to others! And if you think you are fit to be a wise teacher, think again!

Selfish ambition and bitter envy need to be challenged in our hearts, not expressed in our words. Words that flow out of selfish desires always have a toxic effect on relationships.

• *What will we find where such sinful reactions are expressed unchecked (v. 16)?*

This is a far cry from good 'deeds done in the humility that comes from wisdom' (v. 13). Selfish ambition puts my success above your needs. Bitter envy is all about me too. I want what you have and so there is bitterness in my heart towards you. Disordered desires lead to disordered relationships and all sorts of other sins.

Here is a horrible picture of fake 'wisdom' and its fruit. The people speaking and living like this may be in church but this 'wisdom' does not come down from heaven, rather it erupts from our sinful self-centred hearts. James calls it 'earthly, unspiritual, demonic' (v. 15). Strong words! Our sinful desires and the words that express them are tremendously dangerous.

PRAY

Pray that you and your church leaders would live good lives and never harbour bitter envy or selfish ambition.

What does true wisdom look like? James is trying to help his readers distinguish between a false 'wisdom', which he calls 'demonic' (3:15), and true wisdom which 'comes from heaven' (v. 17). As James describes this true wisdom, he doesn't talk about cleverness or gifts or qualifications; he talks about character and life. People may think they are wise and want to be teachers. Such people may sound impressive. But if they are full of selfish ambition and bitter envy, the words of such teachers will be accompanied by 'disorder and every evil practice' (3:16).

Now James tells his readers eight characteristics of the truly wise person. It sounds like a description of the Lord Jesus, the true wisdom that 'comes from heaven' (see 1 Cor. 1:30).

- *It seems that James picks virtues he fears his readers lack! What connections can you see between James' list (vv. 17–18) and his concerns in the rest of his letter?*

Remember the Christian who said to his destitute brother, 'Go in peace; keep warm and well fed' (2:15–16), but did nothing to help him. There was no sincerity or consideration there, or any 'fruit' of good deeds.

Remember the Christian who said to the rich man, 'Here's a good seat for you,' but to the poor man, 'Sit on the floor by my feet' (2:3). We saw no sign there of the mercy and impartiality with which God treats us.

James will go on to talk to his readers about their 'fights and quarrels' (4:1). There seems to be no peace in this dysfunctional congregation.

We might wonder why James says that this heavenly wisdom is 'first of all pure' (v. 17). When we speak of 'pure devotion', we mean that it is wholehearted as well as good. James is concerned that his readers lack such pure devotion to God. He calls them 'double-minded', and from that double-mindedness flow all these other problems, including their false 'wisdom'. No wonder not many of these believers should be teachers! James will call on these believers to 'purify' their hearts (4:8).

- *Teachers in the congregation are 'sowers' of the 'seed' of God's word. What kind of 'sowing' will lead to 'a harvest of righteousness' (v. 18)?*

Teachers need to 'sow in peace'. They need to be peacemakers. They need to give grace as well as talk about it. The life and the words of the truly wise person will always build loving relationships rather than destroy them. How much we need this wisdom!

PRAY

'If any one of you lacks wisdom, you should ask God ...' (1:5). So ask.

 **DAY 28**

This means you!

James says 'you' again and again in the next part of his letter (4:1–10). He becomes very direct with this group of Christians. He will lay bare the heart of what is wrong with this church family.

He begins here with stark words about their relationships. These Christians are at war with each other; James speaks of fights, quarrels, even killing. Not many peacemakers here!

• *What causes these fights (vv. 1–2)?*

When we behave badly in relationships, we tend to blame something or someone else. We may blame our circumstances, or our past, or how the other person has treated us. But James points the finger at our own hearts.

There is an inner battle going on inside each of us. All kinds of desires are fighting to take charge of our outward words and actions (v. 1), and when selfish desires win out, we will treat each other badly.

The desire James mentions here is coveting (v. 2) – wanting what someone else has. We should rejoice in the good gifts that God has given to others, but it sounds as though these believers are simmering with frustrated resentment and jealousy.

Bitter envy turns relationships sour. This shows itself in fights and quarrels and a hatred that is so strong that James likens it to murder – 'you kill', he says (v. 2).

James does not say exactly what it is that these believers want, but the right response to feeling in need is not to fight but to pray.

• *What is wrong with the prayer life of these Christians (vv. 2–3)?*

These believers are acting just like unbelievers. They either aren't praying at all or are only praying thoroughly selfish prayers. In fact, it sounds as if these Christians are just praying for more money to spend on their pleasures (v. 3). Perhaps those who had less were envying the lifestyles of those who had more, and those who had more were wanting yet more still.

God knows our hearts. He knows the motivations that lie behind our requests to him. The pray-ers in verse 3 don't sound in real need, just greedy for more, and so God will not give them what they ask.

These Christians are looking for satisfaction in the wrong place. The unbelieving world runs after wealth and the pleasures it buys, but such things will never bring us lasting fulfilment. There is only one relationship which can bring us that, and putting that relationship right will bring peace to all our other relationships too.

PRAY

Ask God to help you find your satisfaction in knowing him, so that your relationships may be peaceful and your prayers unselfish.

Do you know how much God longs for your undivided devotion?

God cares deeply about how we treat him. James' readers are clearly treating each other badly, but how we treat others actually reflects how we are treating God too. What James has to say now about how these believers are treating God is devastating.

• **What sin does he say they are guilty of (v. 4)?**

Here is the very heart of all that is wrong in this congregation. All through the Old Testament, marriage is used as a picture of the relationship between God and his people. James' Christian readers are married to God but they are currently having an affair with 'the world'. James accuses them of adultery.

Marriage involves an exclusive commitment, a promise to 'forsake all others'. Yet James' readers have fallen in love with the unbelieving world around them and been unfaithful to their spiritual marriage vows.

James is not talking here about Christians having friendships with unbelievers. Jesus was known as 'a friend of … sinners' (Luke 7:34) and we should follow his example. James is speaking here of spiritual adultery

– giving first place in your heart to someone or something other than God.

These Christians' hearts are divided. They are still in church but their first love has become the things of this world – money, success and pleasure.

But God will not share our devotion with anyone else. In his grace and mercy, God gave us his Spirit to dwell in our hearts, and now, like a rightfully jealous husband, God longs for our hearts to return to him (v. 5).

• **These believers are behaving like enemies of God, but there is hope. Why (v. 6)?**

James' readers have already received grace from God in Christ. Spiritually, he gave them 'birth through the word of truth' (1:18), and now God is willing to give these wayward Christians 'more grace'. Their spiritual adultery need not be the end of their story.

The way to receive God's grace has always been the same. In the scriptures there are only two basic categories of people: the proud and the humble. God opposes one and gives favour to the other (v. 6). The humble repent and come to God to receive his grace; the proud do not.

In the coming verses, James will help his readers see how to humble themselves before God. He so wants them to repent and receive again God's grace.

'The way to "up" is down.'

Look at yourselves! That has been James' message to this complacent, worldly, warring Christian fellowship. He has called them spiritual adulterers and enemies of God.

• **What does he now call them (v. 8)?**

James wants these believers to be in no doubt about the spiritual danger they are in. They are double-minded sinners, desperately in need of God's grace.

There is great danger too though in hearing God's word to repent but then doing nothing about it (1:22). So now James calls on his readers in a very direct way to get on and take action. Look at all the action words he uses in these few sentences.

Submit. Resist. Come. Wash. Purify. Grieve. Mourn. Wail. Change. Humble yourselves!

This is not a time for laughing, as if nothing is really wrong. This is a time for weeping and grieving over the sin which will lead to death if we let it flourish unchecked and become full-grown (1:15). Double-mindedness must end. Giving in to temptation must stop. This is a call to come back to God in wholehearted and humble repentance and submission.

• **But James has words of encouragement too. What promises does he give to those who heed his words (vv. 7–8, 10)?**

These believers have got into very bad patterns of behaviour; they have got into the habit of following the devil's encouragements to sin. Perhaps they felt they could never change. But James wants them to see that the devil does not rule them; they can say no to his whispered prompts to curse and envy and fight. Do that, James says, and the devil 'will flee from you' (v. 7). The devil is real and he is evil, but his only power over us is if we choose to pay attention to him!

At the centre of all that James says here is the promise that our broken relationship with God can be restored. This is marvellous good news. Spiritual adultery is not the unforgiveable sin. God will come near to us in grace and favour if we come near to him again, but we need to come humbly, submissively and in deep repentance. If we try to lift ourselves up in pride, we will find that God is against us (4:6).

If we do bow down and humble ourselves before the Lord though, he will not crush us or condemn us; he will lift us up (v. 10).

In the Christian life, 'the way to "up" is always down'.

PRAY

Come near to God again in the way James commands and rejoice in the wonderful promises he gives.

A restored relationship with God will transform our lives and our relationships.

Humble hearts must flow out into humble speech. James has already taught that if you don't 'keep a tight rein' on your tongue, you are deceiving yourself and your religion is worthless (1:26). In this last part of his letter (4:11 – 5:20), James repeatedly calls on his readers to get their tongues under control.

Slander must stop (v. 11), so must boasting (4:16), grumbling (5:9) and swearing (5:12). Instead, James wants to hear wails of repentance (5:1), prayers (5:13–16), songs of praise (5:13), submissive calls to church elders (5:14) and confessions of sin to fellow believers (5:16). In all these ways, what these Christians' claim to believe must flow out into what their tongues actually say.

• *James begins with the issue of slander. These believers must stop speaking against each other, for what are they doing when they speak like this (v. 11)?*

How we talk about each other really matters. We can be very quick to run down our Christian brothers and sisters in our conversations. James' message here is that when we sit in judgment over our fellow believers like this we are actually sitting in judgment over God's word. The Lord Jesus taught his followers, 'Love your neighbour as yourself' (2:8), and so backbiting, negative gossip and the ripping apart of reputations must stop. Speaking in such ways is certainly not loving others in the way Jesus commanded.

If we speak like this, we are acting as if we have the right to disregard our Lord's law of love whenever we like. We need to watch out, for our attitude to his law reveals our attitude to Jesus himself.

• *How does James humble his readers (v. 12)?*

When we slander our Christian brother or sister, we behave as if we have the right to sit over them as their judge and jury. Who do we think we are? There is only one person who has the right to make such laws and judge how well we keep them, and it is not us!

Only God will be the judge in the only judgment that really counts. On the last day he will either destroy us as we deserve or save us through his mercy and grace.

God has been gracious to James' readers who believe in the Lord Jesus. Now he wants them to treat each other with the same mercy and grace. We are to love our neighbour in what we say, not rubbish them!

PRAY

Pray that your words about others would be loving and gracious.

How do you talk about your future plans?

It sounds as if some of James' readers have been speaking exactly like unbelievers (v. 13). They are planning their lives with no reference to God and their goal in it all is making money. James calls their schemes 'arrogant', and he calls the way they speak and boast about these plans 'evil' (v. 16).

• **What truths does James point his readers back to (vv. 14–15)?**

This again is very humbling. We like to believe we are in control of our lives, but the idea that we control the future is a mirage. We cannot be certain what will happen tomorrow. And our life is just a disappearing mist, here for a little while and then gone; it's just the dash between two dates on a gravestone.

So believers should speak very humbly about the future. It is God who decides if we will even wake up tomorrow. We will live another day only if it is the Lord's will. We can make plans for tomorrow, but we need to remember who rules the world – and it is not us; it is God who holds the future.

These Christians need to start thinking about 'the Lord's will', not just their proud selfish plans. They need to keep in mind how they depend on him for their every breath.

James' readers are 'believers in our glorious Lord Jesus Christ' (2:1). They know who is Lord. James wants them to humbly acknowledge his Lordship in how they speak about the future.

James' readers know a lot actually. Their problem is that they have not been doing what they know. This church doesn't seem to be in danger of being deceived by false teachers just now, but they are in danger of deceiving themselves. They are thinking that all is well with their spiritual lives when there are massive gaps between what they claim to believe and how they behave.

Now their 'friendship' with the world needs to be replaced with wholehearted devotion to God. Double-mindedness must end. How these Christians speak and live needs to start consistently reflecting what they claim to believe.

Maybe we have never thought about how our planning and speaking might arrogantly dismiss and ignore God's sovereign rule. But now we know and so we need to act.

- *What does James tell his readers about failing to change (v. 17)?*

We must not sidestep James' challenge here: not doing the good we know we should is sin. This matters to God.

PRAY

Pray you remember how dependent you are on God for everything, and that this would be reflected in your speaking and planning.

Repent, while you still can. 'Now listen, you rich people,' James says (v. 1). What he has to say to them is stark and terrifying. It should make them tremble.

• **What should the rich people he is addressing expect in the future (v. 1)?**

These rich people have a terrible future. Misery will come upon them because it seems these people are sinful, unrepentant and facing the judgment of God, as we shall see. They ought to be weeping and wailing, either in repentance or in sheer terror. It seems unlikely that these rich oppressors are members of the congregation; more likely, James is proclaiming God's verdict on these evil doers so that the believers they oppress are reassured that justice is coming.

These rich people employ workers to harvest their crops, but they fail to pay them (v. 4). Instead, they keep their gains for themselves. They hoard their wealth, living lives of luxury and self-indulgence on earth (v. 5). Their corruption and injustice know no bounds. They have even 'condemned and murdered the innocent one', who was not opposing them (v. 6).

But evil does not go unnoticed and it will not remain unpunished.

• **These rich oppressors may think they have got away with their actions, but they haven't. Why (v. 4)?**

Those who are treated unjustly cry out for justice. It may seem as if no one pays any attention, but the Lord Almighty does; he is amassing evidence for his coming judgment. Those unpaid wages cry out against these rich oppressors too and God takes note of it all.

James puts a very different perspective on the hoarded wealth of the rich and their lavish, self-indulgent lifestyles. The rich may feel pleased to be piling up money, rather than paying the wages they owe. But James pictures hoarded wealth as rotting and corroding (vv. 2–3). In the end, it will do these rich people harm not good. It will be more evidence against them at the judgment, testifying against them. On that day, their hoarded wealth won't just be destroyed; it will destroy them, eating their 'flesh like fire' (v. 3).

These are the 'last days' before God's terrible judgment. Earthly wealth will soon be gone – how foolish not to use it for good while we have the opportunity!

These rich oppressors have every selfish indulgence now, but judgment is coming. As they gorge themselves on luxuries, they are really just like animals unwittingly fattening themselves up ready for a trip to the slaughter house (v. 5). They should wake up and repent, while they still can.

PRAY

Thank God that one day he will judge and end all injustice, and pray that those who live as his enemies would repent and receive his grace before it is too late.

Will you keep trusting and obeying Christ, even through suffering?

Some of James' readers are suffering unjustly. James wants to reassure these believers that one day these wrongs will be righted. The corrupt landowners who have abused them and 'condemned ... the innocent one' (5:6) will be condemned themselves.

• *So what does James call on his Christian brothers and sisters to do (vv. 7–8)?*

When we are suffering unfairly, we want justice right now, today! But James tells his suffering readers that they will have to wait; they must be patient until the Lord comes. They must stand firm in their faith through all the days when God seems to be doing nothing to help them.

James points these believers to the example of the farmer. The farmer plants his seeds and then he too has to wait to receive what he wants. He waits for the seasonal rains his plants need to grow and for the land to produce its valuable crop. Like the farmer, Christians must wait patiently for the 'harvest' that is coming, and it *is* coming. God has promised to give the crown of life to those who love him, who persevere faithfully through their trials (1:12).

The Lord's coming may be anytime; James says it is 'near' (v. 8). So don't give up now, however difficult things seem!

The Lord's coming isn't just an encouragement; it is also a challenge.

• *What must these Christians avoid doing and why (v. 9)?*

It is not just oppression from unbelievers that tests us, as we wait for the Lord's coming. There will also be many reasons we may feel like grumbling against our own Christian brothers and sisters, for, like us, they are far from perfect!

But God hates grumbling – that rumbling, nagging, spreading discontent and criticism we find so tempting, especially when life is hard. God cares about sin inside his church just as much as outside it. James says, 'The Judge is standing at the door!' These believers need to be ready for him.

If you knew Christ was about to walk in, how would you speak of your fellow Christians? God has accepted you despite your many weaknesses and failings. Will you not accept your brother or sister in Christ in the same way? Grumbling against one another is serious and it needs to stop.

Real saving faith must lead to changed lives. God will treat us in the way we treat others – so be gracious!

PRAY

Ask the Lord to help you persevere patiently as you wait for his coming and not to grumble against your fellow believers in the meanwhile.

Being a believer has always been challenging, but the right response to suffering has always been same too. James now encourages his Christian readers by pointing them to the example of some notable faithful believers who have gone before them.

The Old Testament prophets spoke in the name of the Lord and suffered as a result, yet they didn't give up. They patiently persevered, just as James wants his readers to do.

• *At the time of their suffering these prophets probably seemed abandoned by God, but how do James and his readers see them now (v. 11)?*

some appearances to the contrary now, God does care a great deal about his people. He is full of compassion and mercy (v. 11).

James ends both of his sections about patient perseverance (5:7–9 and 5:10–12) with warnings about speech. The issue this time is not grumbling, but swearing. This swearing was a way of underlining that a particular statement was really true by adding the extra line, 'I swear by ...' James says that Christians must not speak like this.

• *What should these believers say instead (v. 12)?*

James is reminding his friends of what they already know. Looking back on these prophets, believers now count these faithful ones as 'blessed', for as James has already said, 'Blessed is the one who perseveres under trial' (1:12).

James then points his readers to another faithful Old Testament believer – Job. They know about Job too. They have heard of Job's perseverance in his suffering and seen in the scriptures what the Lord finally brought about for him.

At the end of all Job's sufferings, God showered blessings on him. That was a picture of how God will bless all his faithful people in the end. For despite

The word of a Christian should need no extra tags added on to guarantee that it is trustworthy. The truth of what we say should never be in any kind of doubt! Just a simple yes or no is all that should be needed.

Grumbling reveals a judgmental, unforgiving heart. Swearing like this is a sign of double-mindedness. Such speech implies a split in our hearts, so that some of our words are trustworthy but others are not.

Don't grumble against one another or 'you will be judged' (5:9). Don't swear or 'you will be condemned' (v. 12). These are very serious warnings. Present sufferings are no excuse for sinful speech. James is warning his readers not to stray away again from humble, single-hearted obedience to God. Remember, 'The Judge is standing at the door!' (v. 9).

PRAY

Thank God that he is full of compassion and mercy, and that he promises to bless believers who persevere faithfully even through suffering.

H ow will we stay close to God? James has called on these believers to come near to God again in repentance (4:8). Now he wants them to stay near to God.

In the final part of his letter James has been telling these believers much about the right way to use their tongues. Humble hearts must lead to humble words. Just as the wrong use of their tongues demonstrated what was wrong with this congregation, now the right use of their tongues must show that they are back on track.

So these believers must not slander or grumble against each other, neither should they boast or swear. Instead they should speak humbly and honestly and lovingly. Their words must build relationships, not tear them down.

Now in the last few verses of all (5:13–20), James focuses on how his readers should speak to God and on how they can help one another stay close to him. One part of what James says in these last verses is easily misunderstood, so we will take time to look at this whole section over four days, to help us see those verses in their context.

- *James begins in verse 13 though with two very straightforward commands. How should these believers respond in their troubles and joys (v. 13)?*

It is easy to forget God in good times. It is easy to give up on God in hard times. James wants his Christian readers to stay close to God whatever happens. Don't run from God when you face trouble; cry to him for help. He is 'full of compassion and mercy' (5:11). Don't drift from God in happy times when all seems well. 'Every good and perfect gift is from above' (1:17), so thank and praise God for all he has given you.

Don't just come near to God; stay near to him.

Next James asks, 'Is anyone among you ill?'(v. 14). As we read on, it looks at first glance as if James is outlining a course of action that will guarantee physical healing now for this ill person. But when we look at these verses carefully in the context of the whole letter, we find a number of points that should steer us away from such a conclusion, especially as we find no other similar promise in the rest of scripture. We will look at this in more detail tomorrow.

We can rejoice though that when the Lord comes, the suffering of all believers will be over. On that day, no Christian will be ill or in trouble and all of us will be joyfully singing songs of praise.

PRAY

If you are in trouble today, pray for help; if you are happy, praise God. Ask God to help you stay near to him, whatever your circumstances.

Real faith is always accompanied by obedient actions.

James is writing to a church which seems very short on obedient actions. Their relationships with God and with one another are in a terrible state. Spiritually, they are supposed to be 'married' to God, but they have been having an affair with the world.

We need to read 5:14–16 in the light of all this. James writes these words to this wayward congregation, and in their case it seems that illness and sin may be linked in an unusual way.

Most sickness is not a direct consequence of a person's particular sin (see John 9:1–3), though obviously choosing some lifestyles may damage your health. Just occasionally though, there may be another connection. Both Jesus and Paul indicate that sometimes sickness may be God's direct judgment on a sinful person or church (see John 5:1–14 and 1 Cor. 11:27–31). James interleaves sin/forgiveness with sickness/healing in an unusual way in 5:14–16 that suggests that in this disobedient congregation some sickness may be God's discipline on them to call them back to himself.

So, if anyone is sick in this church, James says they should call the elders to 'anoint them with oil in the name of the Lord' and pray for them (v. 14). These were probably signs of repentance – consecrating oneself again to God (anointing) and submitting again to the ministry of the teachers of God's word. God will answer this prayer of faith – the sick person will be saved (the literal meaning of 'made well'), raised up and forgiven (v. 15).

• **What is odd about what James says about this sick person's sin (v. 15)?**

James says of this person who was sick, 'If they have sinned, they will be forgiven.' Why does James use the word 'if' here when, of course, everyone sins? It seems again that James is thinking of the particular situation where sickness has been God's discipline on someone's sin. If the illness was a judgment on their sin, then when this sick person repents, God will restore them both physically and spiritually; they will be both healed and forgiven.

James links repentance with healing in the next verse too (v. 16). More on that tomorrow.

Usually getting ill is just one more unhappy consequence of living in a fallen world, and the right response is private prayer and a visit to the doctor. But if you know you are deliberately living in disobedience to God's word and you get sick, then you should repent and do what James says here. If the sickness was God's discipline, he will raise you up. Most important of all though, he will *always* forgive you.

PRAY

Thank God that his discipline, whatever form it takes, is always to lead us back to himself.

How can broken relationships be restored?

James' readers have been an 'adulterous people' (4:4), but spiritual adultery is not new. God's people were in a similar state long ago in the days of the Old Testament prophet Elijah. Back then, God sent a time of suffering, a drought, to discipline his disobedient people and bring them back to himself in repentance (see 1 Kgs. 17–18). God used Elijah's prayers to move these plans forward in remarkable ways – withholding rain for three years and then ending the drought when the people repented (vv. 17–18).

Among James' readers too there seem to be signs of the Lord's discipline on his adulterous people. In their case though, this discipline seems to be taking the form of sickness. But God will always forgive sinners who repent and then the disciplining judgment on them will end. There is always a way back, as we have seen (5:14–15).

• *So what does James call on everyone in this church to do and why (v. 16)?*

These believers have clearly been treating each other badly. Now James wants them to admit that to one another and say sorry. These Christians don't just need to humble themselves before the Lord; they need to humble themselves before one another too. They need to stop grumbling against one another and start praying for each other.

Is there really a way back from such damaged relationships, with God and with others? James wants to reassure his readers that there is. God will answer their prayers, just as he did Elijah's. And where sickness has been a sign of God's discipline, God will take it away, just as he took away the discipline of the drought back then.

• *How does James encourage these Christians to pray (vv. 16–18)?*

When you are in a right relationship with God ('righteous'), you will begin to pray in line with God's purposes, rather than, for example, just asking for more money to spend on your pleasures (4:3). The prayer of such a righteous person really does change things. Elijah himself was not powerful – he was a human being like everyone else – but through Elijah's prayers God did extraordinary things and restored the people of God. God can do the same for this disobedient church; they just need to ask him.

Perhaps you can think of a relationship with someone in your church family that is in a bad state. Go and admit your fault, ask for their forgiveness and start to pray for them. Call on God for help. Prayer is powerful and effective.

PRAY

Pray for those in your own church family, especially for anyone you have fallen out with, and thank God that the 'prayer of a righteous person is powerful and effective' (v. 16).

Now it is your turn!

As James signs off his letter, he calls on his readers to do for each other what has been done for them. He has written to this church which has gone way off course to call them back to humble repentance. Now he wants them to take responsibility for keeping one another safe spiritually too.

- **What exactly does James want these believers to do (v. 19)?**

Wandering from the truth is an apt description of what has been wrong with this church. These Christians have not stormed out of their fellowship. They do not seem to have embraced major false teachings. These believers are still in church; they are still hearing God's word. But their hearts are divided and their behaviour is moving further and further away from the truth they claim to believe. They are moving in a very dangerous direction, because sin matters; if it is allowed to flourish and become full-grown, it will give birth to death (1:15).

These believers seem oblivious to the danger they are in. But James has seen it, and he has written to call them back to humbly submit to the word planted in them that can save them.

Now James wants these Christians to have a ministry like his, and he isn't just referring to the elders here. James says 'someone' (v. 19) and 'whoever' (v. 20); any Christian can bring a wanderer back.

- **How important is it to do this (v. 20)?**

When a person is doing wrong they do not always appreciate someone trying to convince them to change, however sensitively and lovingly it is done. James' readers may have felt like that themselves, at least at first! But James loved his dear brothers and sisters and wanted to save them from spiritual disaster, so he wrote to turn them 'from the error of their way'. Repentance matters that much. So James' readers too must call back any other brother or sister who wanders from the truth.

It will help of course if we are quick to acknowledge, as James does, that 'We all stumble in many ways' (3:2). Every one of us always needs more grace.

But the glorious good news of the gospel is that if believers in the Lord Jesus Christ do turn from doing wrong, God will show 'favour to the humble' (4:6). We will not face the spiritual death we deserve. The Lord will graciously cover over our 'multitude of sins'.

Please keep reminding me!

PRAY

Pray you would look out for others in your church family and love them enough to bring them back if they wander from the truth.

MORE GRACE

Is there hope?

James writes to a Christian fellowship that you probably would not have been keen to join, certainly if you had had any idea of what was going on there. Yet God had begun a work in these brothers and sisters. He had chosen to give them birth through his word of truth (1:18).

Currently though, they were in a real mess. Relationships between believers seem to have been in a terrible state, and this was just a reflection of the state of their divided hearts. These people were in church, but their hearts were far from God and their lives showed it. There were gaps and inconsistencies everywhere between what they claimed to believe and how they lived. Perhaps most dangerous of all, these Christians seemed arrogantly unconcerned and oblivious to the downward spirals of sin they were descending.

Knowing that God had planted his word in these believers' hearts (1:21) does not lead James to sit back. He writes a hard-hitting letter to warn them and to call them back. James wants them to humble themselves again before the Lord and then to persevere

faithfully together until Jesus comes, whatever happens.

James' method is to uncover bit by bit the danger his dear brothers and sisters are in. He begins by speaking mostly in general terms, saying things like, 'anyone who … (1:23)' and 'believers in our glorious Lord Jesus Christ must …' (2:1). But James' aim is to get his readers to look in this mirror he is holding up and see themselves reflected in what he says.

By the time James blazes out starkly and directly, 'You adulterous people' (4:4), these wayward Christians should be ready to respond to his call to weep in humble repentance and draw near to God again. That is God's desire, for, like a rightfully jealous husband, God longs to have his people back, with hearts that are devoted to him alone. A restored relationship with God will always bear fruit in transformed lives. There will be 'a harvest of righteousness' (3:18).

Is there hope for you if you have wandered from the truth? Or if relationships in your church are in a terrible state? The message of James is a resounding, 'Yes!' For wonderfully,

God is always willing to give 'more grace' (4:6). There is always a way back.

God's word here calls us to humble ourselves again before the Lord we love, receive again his grace and begin living differently. Don't just hear God's word, do it!

PRAY

Come near to God again, grieving over your sin and rejoicing in his grace. Thank God that he has promised to give the crown of life to those who love him and who do persevere faithfully. Pray you would do that!

10Publishing is the publishing house of **10ofThose**.
It is committed to producing quality Christian
resources that are biblical and accessible.

www.10ofthose.com is our online retail arm selling
thousands of quality books at discounted prices.

For information contact: **sales@10ofthose.com**
or check out our website: **www.10ofthose.com**